2nd Edition

ESSENTIAL BASS TECHNIQUE

by Peter Murray

T004824

Correspondence:
Peter Murray
c/o Thermidor Music
2938 Dundas St. W., PO Box 70516
Toronto, Ontario, Canada M6P 4E7

email: petermurray@sympatico.ca
web site: www.thermidormusic.com

Editor: Shauna Kennedy
Research and production assistant: Greg Spas
Photography: Nicolas Greenland
Illustrations: Martin Tielli
Back cover photo: Jane Hinton
Design: David Schellenberg

Thermidor logo illustrated by Martin Tielli and designed by Douglas Counter

Thanks to Marian Hebb, Monique Van Remortel, Jim Roberts, Marc Cooper, Laura Murray, Artie Roth, Pattie Kelly, Andrew & Allan, Steve Lucas, Alain Caron, Don Thompson, Peter Cardinali, Christopher Maloney, Bruce Adamson, Barry Green, Bruce MacLean, John and Carlo at West End Offset, Lionel Williams, Justin Abedin, Sergio Sismondo and Glen Reichwein.

This book is dedicated to the memory of Leonard Arwood Harman.

To discuss bass technique on the Internet with players from around the world, visit the Bass Technique Forum at **www.thermidormusic.com**!

For photocopying or other reprographic copying licenses, contact:
CANCOPY, 1 Yonge Street, Suite 1900, Toronto, Ontario, Canada, M5E 1E5
www.cancopy.com / 1-800-893-5777 or (416) 868-1620

ISBN 978-0-634-03267-7

7777 W. BLUEMOUND RD. P.O. BOX 13819 MILWAUKEE, WI 53213

Visit Hal Leonard Online at
www.halleonard.com

TABLE OF CONTENTS

FOREWORD

*T*echnique is a very large and integral part of music. It's how musicians are able to translate the creative and emotional ideas in their heads through their fingers, onto the instrument and through the speakers. Though the original inspiration at the top of that chain is of prime importance, what drips, oozes or floods out of the speaker cones and into awaiting ears at the chain's end is inevitably dependent on technique.

Without a certain technical proficiency only the most basic of musical ideas have a voice on the instrument. There's no problem with simplicity in itself, and there's no denying that some of the greatest music ever heard has been delivered to the world despite large technical inefficiencies. A little emotion, spirit and right-brain energy can go a long way. However, developing technique on the bass guitar, or any instrument, gives you a "free voice" and brings you closer to realizing the sounds in your head. As your technique develops, the range of options of what you can play grows immeasurably. At the end of the day, your brain and soul are always responsible for the end product; but with technical freedom, you can choose your level of sophistication. You can play fast, slow, quiet, loud, smooth, choppy, sad, happy, angry... and change at will. Without technique, you're handicapped. You may have great musical ideas, but without a voice, they're useless.

I wrote this book because I discovered a real need for clear, concise and sensible technical information for bass guitar; and because I found that the material that was available was plagued by three main problems:

Bass educators very often teach technique without giving reasons.

It's the "do this because I do" approach or, worse yet, "do this because I'm experienced and you're not." Great bass players do not always have exemplary technique. Just because what they do works for them, it doesn't mean that it's sound general practice, especially if, as in most cases, they haven't thoroughly analyzed what it is that they do and why they do it. Remember, musicians get famous for their music, not because of their technique or their teaching ability; so any time you watch an instructional video or read an article and the player says, "do this," make sure that they're also presenting logical, practical reasons for doing so before you even consider taking their advice—no matter how famous they are.

Many bass educators cop out and say "do whatever works for you."

While every player's technique ends up being a unique combination of approaches (and everyone has a somewhat different physical construction), that doesn't mean that you have to start from scratch in figuring out how to play. There's no need to re-invent the wheel. Telling beginners, especially, to "do whatever works for you" is not at all helpful. How's a beginner supposed to know what works? Subjectivity, in fact, ends up being a very small part of technique. We're all human beings with two hands and ten fingers, and certain things simply make the most sense. Once you look at each aspect of technique in a detached, analytical way, being prepared to criticize your own playing, you'll find out that the range of subjective application is surprisingly narrow. Any technical approaches not supported by common sense and human biomechanics needn't be taught and will not be found in this book.

Technique is far too often superficially discussed at a condescendingly simplistic level.

Beginners may have no experience on the instrument, but they're not stupid. They can understand common sense as well as experts—in fact, probably better because they're objective. Experienced players tend to be very defensive about their technique, and reluctant to admit that it could be honed in ways that would expand their control of the instrument; they often have technical problems that are deeply ingrained and difficult for them to identify. There seems to be no material available on bass technique that acknowledges the fact that technique isn't just what you learn at your first lesson; it's a long study, and one that deserves to be not only thoroughly addressed by beginners, but carefully revisited by more advanced players.

Faced with what I perceive to be a very poor standard in technical instruction for bass guitar, I decided to consolidate all of the technical information I've gathered through my years of playing and teaching and present it in the clearest way possible. Some of the approaches I advance are somewhat controversial, as I've learned from discussions with many other players, but I stand by them, having spent several years working on this book "looking through the microscope." In any case, I feel it's very healthy to initiate a dialogue on electric bass guitar technique. In the musical world, it's a very young instrument with entirely unique properties, and it deserves careful study.

The technique presented in this book does not represent the *only* way to play, but it does constitute a cohesive approach to the instrument that will guarantee you a "free voice" on the bass guitar. Readers should be aware that exceptions are thickly woven into the fabric of music, and extraordinary circumstances may require unusual technique. I've tried to focus only on the aspects of technique that are relevant to bass playing in general the majority of the time. As a result, there is no mention of using a pick, chording and polyphonic techniques, slapping, tapping, artificial harmonics or other special techniques—only standard finger playing. When exceptions arise, you just have to make sure that you approach the situation intelligently and efficiently.

I'd like to thank the people who facilitated this journey, especially my supportive parents Joan and Tim, and my late grandfather Leonard, who gave me the bass that appears in all of the photos. Credit is due to my student and colleague Greg Spas, who served as a foil for my crazy ideas and a support for my good ones. His help in the research of the book was invaluable. As the cliche goes, "a picture is worth a thousand words," and photographer Nick Greenland succeeded in conveying what words could not. Any style points awarded to this book are largely deserved by the multi-talented designer David Schellenberg, who laid it out for all to see, and the brilliant artist Martin Tielli, whose vivid hand renderings fit the book like a glove. Last but not least is Shauna Kennedy, who edited the book and helped and encouraged in too many ways to mention. Thanks also to my teachers and students past and present; this book is the product of many lessons taught and received.

TO THE READERS

who are left-handed

We live in a right-handed world and, unfortunately, lefties are forced to deal with minority status (you make up approximately 10% of the world's population). It's not your fault—and it's not going to stop you from making great music. It didn't stop Paul McCartney, Doug Pinnick (King's X), Mark White (Spin Doctors) or Colin Hodgkinson (Back Door).

If you're left-handed, you have to either play a left-handed bass and apply a "mirror image" approach to this book, or train yourself to deal with a right-handed bass. The latter challenge has been met most notably by John Patitucci and Mark Egan. Then there's Jimmy Haslip of the Yellowjackets, who plays a right-handed bass upside down, with the bottom string closest to the ground!

If you take the most common route and play a left-handed bass, just remember that everything in this book is backward for you: left is right, right is left, and the pictures only make sense held up to a mirror.

who play fretless bass

Fretless basses don't produce fixed pitches by contacting frets, so they introduce the added challenge of intonation. Players of fretless instruments should be able to use most of the technique presented in this book, with the obvious adaptation of "fret-related" issues. I strongly suggest that beginners develop good technique on a fretted instrument before graduating to fretless, because mastering accurate control of intonation is indeed a formidable task, and not one to be taken lightly.

who play 5-, 6-, 8- or 12-string bass

Although 5- and 6-string basses have become increasingly popular in the last ten years, the vast majority of players still play with frets on four strings (up to 96%, according to a recent poll of *Bass Player* magazine readers). Therefore, I've geared this book to four-string fretted bass players with the hope that fretless, 5-, 6-, 8- and 12-string players will be able to use the relevant information and intelligently adapt the rest.

However, since most of the technique adaptations for 5- and 6-string bass are related to muting issues, I've provided a muting overview for extended-range basses as part of the summary on page 48.

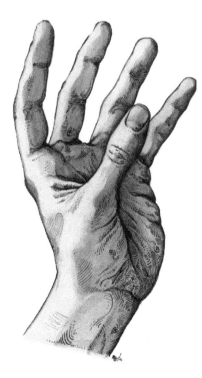

BASIC PRINCIPLES OF **TECHNIQUE**

ECONOMY OF MOTION

Playing the bass requires a complex coordination of muscular activity, mostly in the fingers. With every movement, muscle "work" is done and energy is expended. The more energy you expend as you play, the harder playing is. If you're moving your fingers or other body parts in ways that aren't relevant to the task at hand (playing what you're playing), then you're wasting energy.

Wasting energy has a very detrimental effect on technique. It makes your playing unfocused and inefficient, and puts a ceiling on the complexity and speed of what you can play. In the short term, you'll have a lower capacity for speed ("chops") and in the long term, you'll find yourself lacking endurance. Furthermore, your physical struggles will distract your mind from the music and you'll be less able to concentrate on important things like playing interesting lines, grooving with the drummer and listening to the other musicians.

Great musicians, on any instrument, tend to make their playing look effortless. They can play incredibly complex music and not break a sweat, and their hands seem to glide across the fingerboard with ease. It looks easy because they're only moving as much as they have to—which is usually not a lot. One of the main problems that players tend to have in technique is an excess of physical movement, and you'll notice this issue come up a lot in this book.

A corollary to this issue is "spreading movement out over time." The muscular work that takes place as you play is most efficient when finger movements are gradual and smooth. Sudden movements take a lot more energy and usually result in a sloppier sound.

> *Economy of movement is achieved when, during a given act, those muscles which have nothing affirmative to contribute to its execution remain passive, while those upon which the burden of effort rightfully belongs become active. When muscles which should be passive become active, interfering tensions are introduced. As a result, the body responds awkwardly and inefficiently.*
>
> *Cornelius L. Reid,* **The Free Voice: A Guide to Natural Singing**

- Continuous curved motions are preferable to straight-line motions involving sudden and sharp changes in direction.
- Free, smooth movements (where the muscles initiating movement are unopposed) are faster, easier and more accurate than restricted or controlled movements.
- Rhythm is essential to the smooth and automatic performance of an operation; the work should be arranged to permit an easy and natural rhythm wherever possible.
- Hesitation, or the temporary and often minute cessation from motion, should be analyzed and its cause accounted for and, if possible, eliminated.

    Tufts University, **Handbook of Human Engineering Data**

TONE QUALITY AND CONSISTENCY

One of the most important assets a bassist can have next to musicality, taste and groove ability is good tone quality. Tone is somewhat subjective and there is no specific definition of "good tone", but tonal consistency, or the extent to which your tone is regular, is something that undeniably imparts "quality" to the sound of your playing.

Producing consistent tone and output level is especially important in recording situations. Especially if you're playing something simple such as eighth-note pedals, the notes need a strict regularity in order to fulfil the anchoring function required of them. If the notes all sound different and fluctuate in volume, compression can level them out to an extent, but makes a shoddy replacement for even technique.

Consistency of tone is something that results directly from consistency of movement. So once again, we're back to the first point: if you only move your fingers as they need to be moved, and you do so regularly and smoothly, you'll have a consistent output in terms of both the quality and quantity of sound. This will also increase your control of dynamics and give you the ability to produce a wealth of diverse tonal "colours" or timbres.

Also related to the control of sound is the control of silence. Unless you're playing double-stops or chords, at any given point in time you should be muting three of your four strings. This involves an elaborate muting process involving cooperation between the right and left hands. Many aspects of technique involve muting functions that help ensure that you never mess up your sound with open strings and excessive fret buzzing.

NATURAL MOVEMENT

None of us came out of the womb with a bass in our hands, though some players may seem as if they did. No matter how you slice it, the instrument is a "foreign" object and there are two tasks related to the challenge of making the bass "part of the body": first of all, bass manufacturers must pay attention to the construction of the human body in designing ergonomically-considered instruments. A well-designed bass should feel comfortable. Secondly, the way our fingers and hands and bodies are designed should factor in when figuring out how to play the instrument. We all have the same basic anatomy, and certain generalizations can be made regarding what movements work in concert with human construction, and what movements work against it.

> **biomechanics** deals with the various aspects of physical movements of the body and body members.
>
> **kinesiology** deals with the study of human motions as a function of the construction of the musculoskeletal system.

It's extremely important to always bear in mind that we are all creatures of habit, down to the most minute detail, so we tend to confuse what is "natural" with what is "comfortable." Things that are comfortable are so almost entirely because we're used to them. When things become habitual through repeated application, they start to feel natural because we can't imagine them any other way; but we have to take a few steps back and objectively reassess what we do in order to find out whether our comfortable habits are actually natural and efficient.

Many "overuse injuries" might better be termed "misuse injuries," because they are due to poor movement patterns. Good form and a smooth technique help prevent injury, and even the best performers might benefit from an occasional review. For the injured performer, a change in technique may be more appropriate than any medical intervention. A good technique is consistent and simple. Inconsistent or unnecessarily complicated motion is hard to control and thus invites injury.

Dorothy Bishop, **The Musician as Athlete**

When you develop technique with "natural movement" in mind, you're working efficiently and reducing the likelihood of pain and injury. It's unnatural finger and hand movements that lead to cumulative trauma disorders such as tendinitis and carpal tunnel syndrome. These nasty afflictions develop as a result of long-term repetition of certain activities that lead to an adaptive response within the body. In other words, if you repeatedly subject your fingers and hands to an unnatural mechanical task, your anatomy will eventually rebel, often in very painful and permanent ways.

When trying out a new technique approach, expect it to feel a little odd at first and don't pass judgement on its effectiveness based on that temporary discomfort. If it's derived from common sense and natural manual physiology (as everything in this book is), it will soon feel much more "natural" than your old way of playing.

STRENGTH

A lot of emphasis is often put on muscle strength in bass playing, and the bass is often labelled a "strength instrument." Though it may require more physical strength than many other instruments such as the guitar, you don't have to be a bodybuilder to play. In fact, basses are easier to play than ever, especially if the action on your bass is low (set up with the strings close to the fretboard) and the strings are relatively light. There's nothing macho or productive about making playing hard for yourself; your audience doesn't know, or care, about your action and string gauge. So set up your bass to work with you and not against you for the best musical result.

No other activity in which we engage requires the accuracy, speed, timing, smoothness or coordination of muscular contraction exhibited in finished musical performance.

*Frank R. Wilson, **Tone Deaf and All Thumbs***

Hand exercises, finger grips and weight training may be marginally beneficial to your playing, but are a waste of time compared to practicing bass playing. In fact, those exercises can even work to your disadvantage by developing certain muscles disproportionately to others that are used in bass technique. For example, finger-grips with springs exercise the flexor muscles of the fingers but not the extensors (the springs do that work for you), so they exercise only half of the muscles involved.

If you're training for a marathon, you do so by running. Music's no different in that the training should be practical and directly relevant. To build strength in the naturally weak left-hand pinky, for example, simply practice exercises on the bass that require it. To warm up before a gig, play your bass. Nothing prepares you better for musical situations than practicing music.

CHOPS AND THE CHOPS "RESERVOIR"

"Chops" is the popular term given to the capacity for playing fast. I often describe chops as a supply of ability which is limited, but almost never used in its entirety. Chops isn't just for speed-demons—you really need more chops than you normally use, because if you're playing "full out" all the time, you won't have any endurance at all. You'll put yourself at risk of injury, always require warm-ups and be unable to perform satisfactorily anytime a little distraction comes up. If you're tired, in a bad mood, cold, hungry, stressed or injured, your playing will immediately suffer; but if you have a reservoir to draw from, you'll be able to play consistently well under almost any circumstance, and that's one of the marks of a true professional. Developing efficient technique is essential for building up chops and a "chops reservoir," because speed relies entirely on efficiency.

FACTORS RELATED TO TECHNIQUE

Stress

Any kind of stress or unproductive tension, mental or physical, is an enemy of good technique. It's important to be relaxed when you play, because only then can your fingers operate efficiently. Laboured breathing, anxiety, stage-fright and even intense moods of depression or anger can debilitate your technique by distracting your brain and robbing you of focused, positive energy.

String Action

"Action" refers to the distance between the strings and the fretboard. When the action on your bass is set low, it's easier to play because the fingers don't have to work as hard to press the strings down against the frets. Setting the action too low, however, tends to result in a lot of fret buzzing because the strings and frets are so close. A professional technician should be able to set up any decent bass to be easy to play and free of excessive fret buzzing.

Gauge of Strings

How light or heavy your strings are is a highly subjective matter. Generally speaking, lighter strings are easier to play and more "pliable," but not quite as thick in bottom-end tone. On the other hand, heavier strings tend to have better sustain and bass impact, but can be considerably harder to play. Therefore, some compromise is necessary. I usually recommend light strings because they don't restrict your technical options, but I would suggest trying a variety of different gauges and finding something that you feel comfortable with, both sonically and from a "feel" standpoint.

Weight and Weighting of the Bass

The instrument needs a certain weight to it in order to feel substantial in your hands and in order to produce a good tone, but basses that are too heavy can cause excessive strain on the shoulders and as a result, general fatigue. Some instruments have a good weight but bad weighting; in most cases, badly-weighted basses are "neck-heavy" and place an additional and unnecessary burden on the left hand just to hold up the neck. "Body-heavy" basses pull hard on the shoulders and require the left hand to pull the neck down. A properly weighted bass should remain "in position" when you stand up and take both hands away from the instrument.

Standing and Sitting

Bass players usually perform standing up and need to be able to play comfortably in that position, but I usually recommend sitting as an optimal position for practicing. It allows you to be relaxed just that little bit more by taking the weight off your shoulders and legs, which means you'll be able to practice for longer and absorb yourself more deeply in what you're working on.

Size of Hands and Length of Fingers

Bass players come in all shapes and sizes. Many of those who have smaller hands lament the fact and fear that their short fingers will be unable to make the necessary stretches that bass technique demands. Though finger length can have some effect on reach, with proper training, developing the more important abilities of flexibility and coordination will let you more than make up for it (you should see the stubby hands that 6-string bass virtuoso Anthony Jackson has). Whatever you do, don't debilitate yourself by dwelling on things that you see as being restrictive and unavoidable problems. Not only do you have no choice other than to deal with what you've got, but you will also find that such problems can be easily overcome with a little willpower and hard work.

Hearing

Neuromuscular control has to do with the way that your brain gives directions to your muscles, which in turn perform mechanical tasks. When those directions are carried out, the senses send a message (sort of like a progress report) back to your brain to let it know how it's doing and what may be changed in order to improve the results. The most important sense in this feedback loop is that of touch, but hearing is also involved. When you can't hear yourself because of bad monitoring, a weak amplifier, damaged hearing or a combination of these things, you are unable to have refined control of the tone you are generating. So I suggest obtaining a sufficiently powerful amplifier, positioning it so that you can hear it clearly at reasonable volumes and, as much as possible, protecting your hearing by wearing earplugs at loud concerts. The best arrangement I've found is to keep stage levels low and perform without earplugs for maximum clarity of hearing, but wear earplugs when in the audience.

Alcohol and Drugs

Though you need to be relaxed and "loose" for optimal performance, alcohol and drugs provide illusory help. One drink may take the edge off your nerves, but one drink too many will seriously compromise your coordination and even worse, will impair your judgement about how well you're playing. You may think you're wailing, but your audience may think otherwise. So to be safe, for the good of your music, play sober.

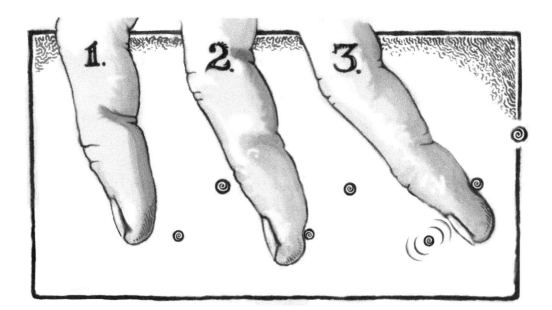

THE STUDY OF **TECHNIQUE**

FOR BEGINNERS

Anyone taking up the bass guitar must first be inaugurated into the bass world with some basic technical instruction. Even if you've never learned a thing about theory and harmony, you could make a lot of music with only some technical background and your two ears.

Perhaps the best reason to learn technique as early as possible is because of the nature of the learning process itself. Since music is an art and a form of self-expression, creative ideas and emotions are of prime importance; but in order to allow for a free flow of those internal intangibles, things like technique and theory have to be rendered second-nature, or ingrained. The last thing you'll want to worry about on a gig or in rehearsal is whether you're alternating fingers or not, or whether you're muting the A string with your right-hand pinky while playing on the G string. You want to be thinking about music; in fact, you probably want to be feeling, emoting and reacting more than thinking.

How do you get to that stage? How do you internalize good technique to the point where it kicks in every time you play? Well, it's a long process. For the majority of players, most of the process is rarely conscious. Few get enough technical training early on to help maximize the proportion of good habits to bad habits. Most go on blind to the intricacies of technique—though hopefully, if their instincts are good, they develop enough functional ability to give some voice to their musicality.

Far preferable to that approach is knowing and understanding what you're doing right from the start. If you learn good technique from square one, you have a clean slate and the opportunity to develop only good habits. This is a lot easier than trying to change bad habits that have been ingrained through years and years of playing. So, beginners take heart. In many ways you have an upper hand, and this book should give you an even further advantage.

FOR INTERMEDIATE PLAYERS

Say you've been playing for a few years and you consider yourself to have a fair control of the instrument. You can play, but you still don't feel that what's coming out of the speakers matches what's coming out of your head. Certainly most players fall into this category.

You should consider the likelihood that inefficient technique is responsible for a large amount of this blockage. Maybe you can't play as fast as you want, or you get physically sore after playing for an hour and a half. Maybe your sound is less consistent than you want it to be.

All of these things can be cured by diagnosing your technique difficulties (with the aid of this book) and treating them with concentrated, specific exercises which isolate the problems and focus your attention on them. Either you or your bass teacher has to make the diagnosis, and it's up to you to find the patience and diligence to fix the problem. Learning technique through "forcible ingraining" is not easy. But it's the only way to change if you want to replace inefficient habits with sensible, focused ones.

FOR ADVANCED PLAYERS

Advanced players tend to be where they are because they've developed a level of control that matches their mature musical personality. They have the technique required to execute the music that they want to play. They don't feel trapped by their fingers, and whatever passes through their head has some kind of a voice on the instrument and finds its way into the music.

However, music is a journey, not a destination; and very few advanced players have completely efficient technique. Theoretically, if you can play what you want to play, you have good technique—although over time your musical ideas may become influenced by your ability to express them technically.

Therefore, even advanced players can grow musically if they're able to re-subject themselves to technical self-criticism. Obviously, you have to really believe that you stand to gain something in order to go through the sometimes painful process of self-analysis.

Intermediate and advanced players should understand that any technique work will temporarily slow them down and cause some disorientation. But it's one step back, three steps forward. Think of it as an investment in your ability to play without restraints.

PRACTICING **TECHNIQUE**

Practicing, in general, is a highly underrated skill. It's an art in itself and one that few achieve mastery of. You can be sure that any great musician you can think of attained greatness through many hours and years of practice. We don't think of our bass heroes as sitting in the basement alone, spending time on such a lowly thing as practicing. But they did, and we are witnesses only to the fruits of their labours.

TOOLS

It's difficult to "teach" the art of practicing, largely because it's inevitably a very personal thing. It consists mostly of a self-motivation and self-organization process that has to suit the personality and lifestyle of the individual. Having said that, however, there are general tools and practicing ideas that make a great deal of sense and deserve being tried.

The first thing is **state of mind**; and this counts for almost everything. Without a positive, patient and conscientious attitude, practicing is futile. You have to find the motivation deep inside to allow you to mentally focus on what you're doing, and more specifically, the things that you know you have to work on. It's very unproductive to sit down with your bass and aimlessly noodle through your favourite licks. Furthermore, you'll likely just be further ingraining the bad habits you've developed. If you want to improve, you quite simply have to identify tasks, make a plan of attack and get busy. The more you can get inside what you're doing and concentrate, the more you'll benefit from practice.

Time and place are also important considerations for practicing. You have to deal with whatever time is available to you—and don't let yourself be told that you have to put in eight hours a day in order to get anything out of the instrument. Quality is infinitely more important than quantity, and it's amazing what you can accomplish in as little as half an hour. It's better to practice effectively for an hour a day than to practice for seven hours once a week. The place where you practice should be well-lit, adequately heated and as quiet and secluded as possible. You should practice with an amp when available, because hearing your playing amplified keeps you in touch with your control of tone and muting. Sitting in an ordinary hard chair is best, because couches and soft chairs tend to put your body in odd positions and standing up tends to be tiring and distracting. Telephones, televisions, significant others, kids, parents and siblings should all be very much avoided.

A **metronome** and a **timer** are extremely useful tools. The metronome, or any timekeeping device such as a drum machine, is important because it not only ingrains good time feel, but also serves as a disciplining agent. Certain things need to be practiced slow, and a metronome keeps you roped in. When you're applying your technique to chops development, the metronome keeps you pushing yourself. Several years ago, a friend imparted to me the hidden virtues of the generic kitchen electronic egg timer. One problem with practicing is that the brain has a nifty way of making one minute feel like ten when you're practicing something as tedious as major scales; but with a simple little beeping timer you can decide to practice something for four minutes, set the timer and immerse yourself completely until the four minutes are up and the beeper goes off. You'll be surprised at how long four minutes really is. The other benefit of this is that it allows you to plan your practice time very thoroughly.

This leads us to **lists** and **practice schedules**. The more organized you are, the more you will get out of your practice time. When you sit down to practice, make a list of the things that you need to work on. Divide the time that you have to practice between those things—for example, four items at 15 minutes each make up roughly an hour of practicing. You'll get much more done and get more satisfaction in far less time if you can make up a specific, realistic plan and do what you set out to do. Afterwards, you can reward yourself with something less structured like learning licks or jamming with a favourite CD.

PRACTICING TECHNIQUE

Technique is something that most players find difficult to focus on while they're playing. If they start thinking about what they're doing, all of a sudden they find themselves screwing up. This is something you just have to deal with. If you're lucky, you can find a good teacher who can watch what you're doing and make critical evaluations of your technique; or, if you have a video camera, maybe you can film yourself and watch back with a little more distance. In many cases, you may be armed only with this book, a bass and your brain.

The first step is to read through this book a step at a time, with your bass. You have to understand the concepts before you can work them into your playing. Play simple things, watch yourself carefully and compare what you're doing to the techniques presented. How do they match up? Are you consistently on track? Sometimes? Never? If you're consistently on track, great. If you're sometimes happening and sometimes not, likely that particular aspect of technique is not ingrained. If it were ingrained, you would be doing it all the time without even thinking about it. So you'll have to figure out how to do it properly and practice it in isolation with intense concentration, forcibly ingraining it. If you're never doing it, ask yourself why. Do the reasons presented make sense to you? If yes, then start working. If no, then write me a letter.

Playing the bass, or any instrument, requires a certain amount of coordination because you're doing so many things at once. I usually liken it to learning how to drive standard. At first, you've got all of these things to think about: the gas pedal, the gear shift, the clutch, the brake, the rear-view mirror... all of which have to be used together quite specifically. So what happens first? You stall the car. But you try it again and again, and after practicing with concentration, you're able to not only start the car, but drive in circles around the parking lot. Eventually, you can speed down the highway, scan for radar traps, be your own DJ on the car stereo, chew gum, ogle pedestrians and discuss philosophy or soap operas with your passenger. So it is with bass. At first, you can barely play a note but eventually, you can rule the lower frequencies while careening across a stage, doing windmills, stage-diving, ogling screaming fans and/or dodging rotten vegetables.

The aim of technical study, whether elementary or advanced, should be to get the playing apparatus into such a condition of efficiency that it functions unconsciously, the conscious mind being thus freed to concentrate on interpretation. A stock of technical ability is gradually built up and stored away, to be drawn on as and when needed.

William Lovelock,
Common Sense in Music Teaching

One can only be free if the essential technique of one's art has been completely mastered.

Nadia Boulanger,
Master Teacher Nadia Boulanger

Obviously, you have to be conscious of your technique before you can make it subconscious. You have to learn about why you're doing what you do, how you're doing it, when you're doing it—and for an unspecified amount of time (as long as necessary), remain conscious of it until you don't have to police yourself anymore. Eventually, you can just follow your instincts, but the idea of this approach is to educate your instincts with efficiency, so that when you do run on "auto-pilot," you're not limited by your technique in any way.

If you're a **beginner**, this will obviously take some time. Technique develops over years and years, and you have to dive in with equal amounts of diligence and patience. What are those clichés that we all hate hearing so much? "You only get out what you put in," "Practice makes perfect"—yeah, yeah. But they're true, and there does have to be some reward for those who are able to log those multitudes of productive hours. Read through this book cover to cover and then go back and look over each section individually and carefully. As you improve, you'll be able to focus more and more on specific problem areas—but be prepared for an uncomfortable "juggling" sensation for a while.

If you're an **intermediate** player, make sure that you don't get smug. Technique is never a closed chapter; and fixing the inefficiencies in your playing will greatly benefit your tone, chops, endurance and dexterity. You may be doing many things well on the instrument, but your task is to seek out those things that could be improved and focus on them. I believe it's as important to know what you're doing right as it is to know what you're doing wrong, and hopefully there will be some positive reinforcement in store for you as well.

If you're an **advanced** player, use what you can. You need a fair amount of willpower in order to re-enter the technical tent, to slip yourself into a saline solution on a slide and under the microscope. If you think of your technique as being infallible, you're probably not reading this book; but if you're interested in tweaking and fine-tuning your technique for maximum performance, read the book as a whole and work through the ideas and pointers that you find relevant. If nothing else, use this book as an excuse to get you thinking about technique in general, and how your playing in particular is shaped by the habits you now hold.

DIVIDE AND CONQUER

As has already been mentioned, it's a waste of time to practice the things you do well. You have to diagnose your problem areas, using this book as a guide, and then focus on those things individually, one at a time. The squeaky wheel gets the grease, and since being conscious of your technique is necessary in order to effect the ingraining process, it makes the most sense to practice specific exercises that don't require your mental attention to be divided between many different coinciding "digital activities."

In other words, don't practice alternating fingers in the right hand while your left hand is struggling through John Coltrane transcriptions. No doubt you would be so preoccupied with the fingerings of the left hand that the right hand fingers, out of necessity, would be all but ignored. Although you would be developing many other aspects of playing, it wouldn't do much to achieve your chosen goal of ingraining solid right-hand fingering.

The extent to which the ingraining process has been successful can be easily tested with the aid of a teacher or an objective third eye. Right-hand technique, for example, can be tested by playing something especially challenging to the *left* hand. So much attention will be required to monitor the activities of the left-hand fingers that the technique in the right hand should be a good indication of what has been ingrained.

USING THIS BOOK

Nobody could reasonably suggest that there's only one way to play the bass guitar—and great music, the desired result, is always the bottom line. However, this book is not about how to generate great musical ideas, it's about how to voice them. It's about mechanics and tools. It's about objectively discovering what factors deserve inclusion in everyone's technique by virtue of their efficiency. Therefore, the techniques that are presented are only included because there's a reason for them; they're the result of a productive combination of practical experience and logical analysis.

Every aspect of technique requires justification or shouldn't be taught. You should work towards ingraining the technique detailed in this book because it makes sense, not because it's in print.

It's very important to understand the reasoning behind technique; grasping the concepts in this book will give you the tools to intelligently deal with the multitude of exceptions and unusual playing situations that will inevitably come up in your musical career.

I've presented this book in a "What? How? Why?" format emphasizing the logical, even scientific derivation of technique. The "whats" are simply the elements of technique (thumb position, finger/string contact, etc.); the "hows" describe clearly the method that should be used to execute those elements; and the all-important "whys" explain the reasons for the methods and how those methods will benefit your playing.

Topics are generally presented in order of importance, but their sequence should not be given too much weight. Even seemingly minor technical details can have large repercussions, so

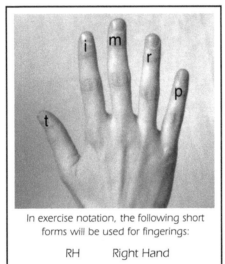

In exercise notation, the following short forms will be used for fingerings:

RH	Right Hand
LH	Left Hand
t	Thumb
i	Index
m	Middle
r	Ring
p	Pinky
∅	Not recommended

it's not enough to just focus on the first few elements. Readers will have to establish their own priorities based on their own weaknesses. For example, if thumb position is something that you have under control, it won't be top priority for you, despite the fact that it's presented first in this book.

For many technique ailments I've included prescriptions. If you have difficulties with a particular aspect of technique, you should deal with it in isolation, applying diligent concentration until the method has been ingrained and no longer requires conscious vigilance. The exercises I've presented isolate the specific element, allowing you to focus instead of scattering your mental energies.

Since everything you play involves technique, theoretically anything can be used to practice it; but I suggest that in addition to the specific prescribed exercises you invest time in practicing staples such as scales and arpeggios. They may seem boring and tedious, but they have great relevance to music in general. To be even more practically relevant, you will have to go back to your repertoire and do a certain amount of re-learning, applying your new technique to songs and licks that you've been playing for ages. You may encounter a certain amount of frustration for a while as you struggle to apply good technique without making a mess of the groove, but trust me, the struggle will pay off in spades.

One more thing—practice in your head when you're away from the bass. The more vividly you can visualize technique, the more easily you will be able to physically apply it. Remember, it's your brain that's telling your fingers what to do, so it's not enough to train your fingers, you have to *train your brain*.

RIGHT HAND

THUMB POSITION

a) The thumb rests on the E string against the pickup (neck side) during play on the G and D strings.

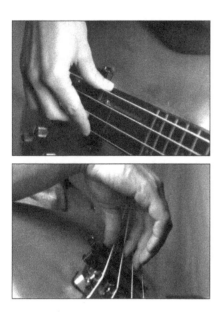

> ♪ This corner provides a secure and comfortable anchor for the right hand because the thumb is naturally angled towards it.

> ♪ Mutes the E string.

b) The thumb rests on the upper left-hand corner of the pickup (neck side) during play on the E string. In the case of basses with two pickups, either pickup may be used.

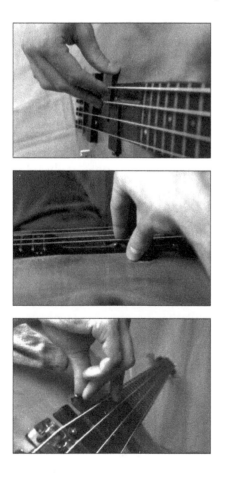

> ♪ This corner of the pickup serves as a secure and comfortable anchor for the right hand because the thumb is naturally angled towards it.

> ♪ In this position, the thumb provides a contact point for the index and middle fingers, establishing a consistent distance that the fingers move with every stroke.

> ♪ The distance between the E string and the thumb in pickup position is the same as the distance between strings (G-D, D-A, A-E).* Therefore, when the fingers are stopped by the thumb in pickup position, they're moving the same distance as they do when playing on the other strings. This leads to a consistency of finger movement from string to string and, in turn, consistency of tone between strings.

c) The thumb rests either in pickup or E string position when playing on the A string.†

♩ Allows the transition between thumb positions (a) and (b) to be gradual, not sudden. This contributes to ease of playing, fluidity and consistency of tone.

†[NOTE: When playing passages of music not involving the E string, rest the thumb on the E string, even during the playing of the A string.

When playing passages that use only the A and E strings, or that involve alternating between the E string and upper strings (such as octave lines on E and D strings or tenths on the E and G strings), keep the thumb anchored on the pickup.

In situations ascending or descending on the D, A and E strings, change thumb position gradually while playing on the A string (see d).]

---

* Though it could be argued that the pickup wasn't designed to be a thumb rest, it just so happens that most basses have their pickups in a position logically suited to accommodate the thumb and provide for a continuity in finger movement between playing on the E string and playing on the other strings.

Some basses have the pickup positioned with the top edge too far from the E string, including the Peavey Dynabass, the Peavey Foundation Series and Tune TWB basses. Many have the pickup positioned too close to the E string to serve as an effective thumb rest: Peavey TL, Rickenbacker 4001 and 4003, Yamaha RBX, G&L L5000 and G&L Climax, Tune SS-2E and James Tyler basses, to name a few.

Yet other basses have peculiar problems related to thumb position and pickup placement: Many Hofner 'Beatle' basses have the neck pickup too close to the fretboard to use as an anchor. The Yamaha Attitude bass has no room between pickups and the pickup is too flush with the pick-guard to provide a stable anchor spot.

Some basses have "thumb-rests" built-in, especially many old Fender models. Invariably, these are not logically placed and luckily, they can usually be easily unscrewed and removed. Some of these models even have a rest for the fingers just past the G string, to stabilize the hand for playing with the thumb! Another example of a thumb-rest is on the Godin acoustic bass guitars, where there's a long, thin rest which runs closely parallel to the E string. The problem is that when resting on it, you're not muting the E string and when playing on the E string, it's too close, so you can't use it as an anchor.

If you're buying a bass, remember to check this distance. If you already play a bass that wasn't designed with this issue in mind, you might consider installing a metal, plastic or wood "thumb-rest" under the strings that rises above the E string by the same distance that separates the other strings from each other.

[NOTE: The position of the thumb determines where the strings are being played by the index and middle fingers. Playing on some areas of the string, for example close to the neck, requires a compromised thumb anchor, so I suggest that you ingrain the pickup anchor as a standard position for the majority of playing situations. Once that is second nature you may occasionally want to play certain parts on different areas of the string for different tone colours.]

d) The thumb slides down the neck side of the pickup when changing between position (a) and position (b).

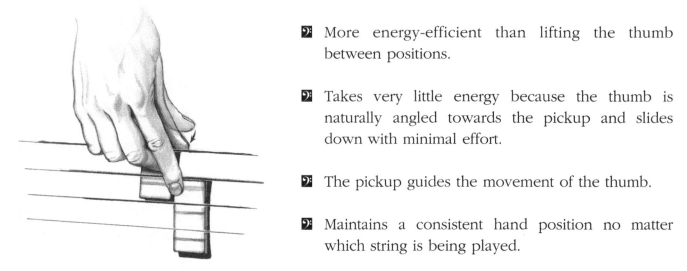

🎵 More energy-efficient than lifting the thumb between positions.

🎵 Takes very little energy because the thumb is naturally angled towards the pickup and slides down with minimal effort.

🎵 The pickup guides the movement of the thumb.

🎵 Maintains a consistent hand position no matter which string is being played.

e) The thumb is anchored securely, but exerts no more pressure than is required to fulfil its function.

🎵 Solid contact is required to firmly anchor the hand and ensure control of finger movement. However, pressing forcefully with the thumb does nothing but waste energy.

f) The thumb should be positioned mostly perpendicular to the body of the bass, pointing down into the instrument.

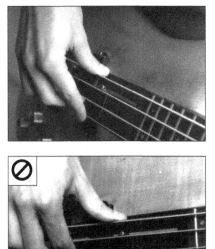

🎵 Angling the thumb in any way parallel to the instrument interferes with the natural "opposable thumb" movement (see *The Opposable Thumb*).

g) The thumb should never be anchored on any string other than the E string.

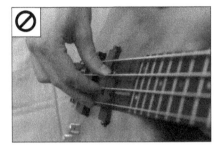

🎵 Lifting the thumb to change position from string to string requires an unnecessary expenditure of energy and compromises fluidity of finger movement.

🎵 The thumb is not required for the muting of the G, D, and A strings (see *Finger Technique* d, *Left-Hand Muting* and the Muting Summary on p. 48).

EXERCISE: *THUMB POSITION & TRANSITIONS*

In order to focus on the thumb position, practice one-octave diatonic scales off the E string (i.e., G major, A♭ major, A major, etc.). In each scale, the thumb position should change from the pickup to the E string **while** you're playing on the A string. Practicing scales off the A string is not useful for practicing this transition since it doesn't involve both thumb positions.

THE OPPOSABLE THUMB

Definition: an arrangement found only in primates whereby the thumb can be brought into a position facing the other digits.

a) In bass technique, the thumb serves as a natural focal point for finger movement, with the playing fingers moving toward the opposable thumb with every stroke.

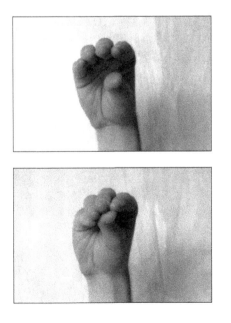

🎵 Moving the fingers toward the thumb is the most energy-efficient and natural finger movement.

b) When the thumb is resting on the upper left-hand corner of the pickup and the E string is being played, the fingers are stopped by the thumb with every stroke.

🎵 The thumb is a natural focal point for finger movement.

🎵 The thumb provides a contact point for the index and middle fingers, establishing a consistent distance that the fingers move with every stroke.

🎵 The distance between the E string and the thumb in pickup position is the same as the distance between strings (G-D, D-A, A-E) (see *Thumb Position*). Therefore, when the fingers are being stopped by the thumb in pickup position, they're moving the same distance as they do when playing on the other strings. This leads to a consistency of finger movement from string to string and, in turn, consistency of tone between strings.

c) When playing on the E string, both index and middle fingers are stopped by the same end-area (or "ball") of the thumb.

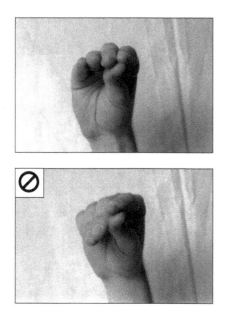

🎵 Stopping all fingerstrokes with the same part of the thumb creates a consistency of movement between the index and middle fingers, which in turn leads to consistency of tone from note to note.

d) When the thumb is resting on the E string, the fingers move directly toward the thumb with every stroke. To achieve this, the neck edge of the "anchor" pickup can be used as a guideline to keep the fingers playing in a standardized area of the strings. The index should be positioned just to the left of this line/edge and the middle finger just to the right.

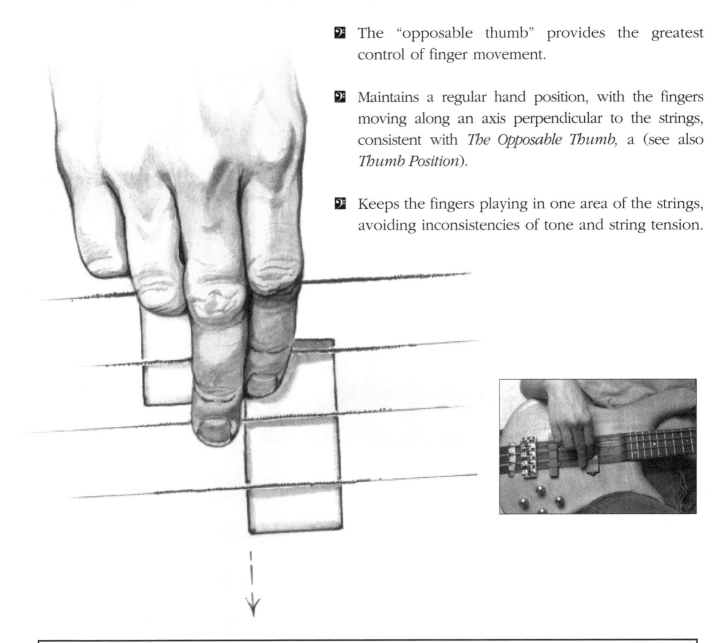

𝄢 The "opposable thumb" provides the greatest control of finger movement.

𝄢 Maintains a regular hand position, with the fingers moving along an axis perpendicular to the strings, consistent with *The Opposable Thumb*, a (see also *Thumb Position*).

𝄢 Keeps the fingers playing in one area of the strings, avoiding inconsistencies of tone and string tension.

EXERCISE: *THE OPPOSABLE THUMB*

For contact - Play eighth-notes on the open E string with your thumb resting on the top of the pickup, stopping every fingerstroke. The fingers should be moving the same distance with every stroke, being stopped consistently by the end-area of the thumb.

For direction of finger movement - Play diatonic scales off the A string, keeping the fingers moving towards the thumb with every stroke. The index should be just to the left (neck-side) of the neck edge of the "anchor" pickup, and the middle finger should be positioned just to the right of that edge.

FINGER TECHNIQUE

a) The ball of the finger (approx. ½ cm or ¼ in. from the very tip of the finger) makes contact with the string during play.

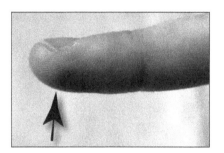

▶ Playing with the very tip forces the finger to be very rigid to ensure accurate and consistent contact with the string. This involves an unnecessary strain and expenditure of energy, sacrificing tone quality, tonal consistency and accuracy. Playing a little further down the finger allows for more relaxed movement.

▶ Playing too far into the finger creates unnecessary friction which results in less control and slower movement.

▶ Finding the right contact point and using it consistently plays a large role in the production of rich, strong tone.

b) A consistent contact point must be maintained as the index and middle fingers stroke the strings.

▶ Tone varies depending on which part of the finger plays the string. A regular contact point therefore contributes to consistent tone.

▶ Consistent finger movement also requires less energy and therefore contributes to control, chops and stamina.

c) The index and middle fingers move in a steady, cyclical motion.

▶ Spreading out movement over time and avoiding sudden or jerky actions is naturally more relaxed and saves energy. In turn, it leads to greater control, consistency of tone, good tone quality, chops and stamina.

Continuous curved motions are preferable to straight-line motions involving sudden and sharp changes in direction.

Tufts University, **Handbook of Human Engineering Data**

d) The playing finger comes to rest on the next string with every note played.

> 🜊 Mutes the next string, preventing accidental vibrations.

> 🜊 Creates a regular distance that the fingers move with every stroke, leading to consistency of tone, chops and endurance.

e) When playing on the E string, the fingers are stopped by the thumb with every stroke.

> 🜊 (see *The Opposable Thumb*, b & c)

f) Fingernails should be kept short, at least on the index and middle fingers.

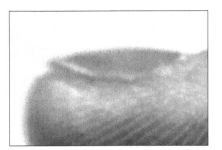

> 🜊 Long fingernails introduce a "tick" noise to your sound which is virtually impossible to produce consistently. It therefore becomes an intermittent noise that detracts from both the quality and consistency of your tone. If you like that sound and want to achieve it consistently, you may want to try playing with a pick.

DIRECTION OF FINGER MOVEMENT

The index or middle finger is drawn across the string until it naturally comes to rest on the next string.

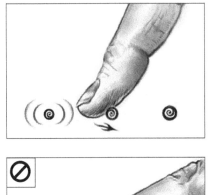

> 🜊 When the finger plays across the string (in a "dragging" motion), it causes string vibrations parallel to the frets, encouraging more free vibration, better tone and less noise.

> 🜊 If the finger plays from above, the string is made to vibrate up and down, creating unwanted vibrations against the frets. This causes fret noise, bad tone quality and reduced sustain.

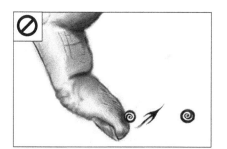

♩ If the fingers play the string from underneath (in a plucking motion, also known as "free-style" in classical guitar technique), they are in a curled and unnecessarily tense position. They don't conform to the efficient "opposable thumb" movement, they don't mute the next string and they can't move consistently since they're not being stopped by the next string with every stroke. Playing the string from underneath also creates up-and-down vibrations and fret noise (as previously described).

FINGER DISTANCE FROM THE STRINGS

The index and middle fingers should stay within a ½ cm or ¼ in. distance from the string being played.

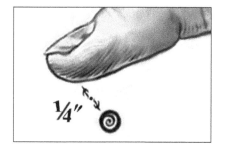

♩ Moving further than this distance above the string results in a greater expenditure of energy and therefore compromises control, tonal quality & consistency, speed and endurance.

♩ Strength/quality of tone is the result of pressure applied by the finger against the string during contact, not the result of momentum of the finger against the string. Therefore, no "wind-up" is necessary.

♩ Moving the fingers further than necessary above the string makes finger movement more "up and down" and leads to excessive fret/string contact and fret noise (see *Direction of Finger Movement*).

♩ Having the fingers regularly positioned any closer to the string would interfere with the free vibration of the string and make playing difficult.

EXERCISE: *FINGER DISTANCE FROM THE STRINGS*

You can help train your fingers to keep close to the strings by playing eighth-notes on an open string, while you bring your left-hand fingers over in front of the bass to rest above the right-hand fingers. Lower your left hand as far as you can without preventing the right-hand fingers from playing. This should help get your right-hand fingers used to keeping movement to a minimum.

FINGER PRESSURE

The index and middle fingers should exert just enough pressure on the string to produce a solid, uniform tone.

> **𝄢** Applying too much pressure wastes energy and also deteriorates tone.

> **𝄢** Applying not enough pressure produces a thin and inconsistent tone.

> [NOTE: The more control one has of tonal consistency, the easier it is to vary finger pressure for playing with dynamics; in other words, controlling volume with the fingers]

EXERCISE: *FINGER TECHNIQUE/PRESSURE/DIRECTION*

To practice finger technique, ignore your left hand and just have the right hand play slow eighth-notes on open strings. Ask yourself these questions:

- Are you dragging your fingers across the string and muting the next string with every note you play?
- Are you using the correct part of the fingers to contact the string?
- Are you applying enough pressure to get a solid tone, but not so much that you're wasting energy?
- How consistent is your finger movement?
- How consistent is your tone?

ALTERNATING FINGERS

Alternate between the index and middle fingers when playing on any string.

> **𝄢** Alternating fingers conserves energy since work is evenly shared between the index and middle fingers. This allows for greater control, consistent tone and good tone quality, and contributes to chops and endurance.

RAKING

Consecutive notes on descending adjacent strings (i.e., G to D or D to A) can be played with a single stroke of the index or middle finger. Both fingers are equally involved in raking.

🎝 When descending strings, this fingering technique is more fluid than alternating fingers, since only one finger movement (a single stroke) is required for the playing of both notes.

[NOTE: In advanced techniques, more than two strings can be 'raked'.]

🎝 Playing the first note puts the finger in contact position to play the second note.

🎝 Raking avoids a "jackknife" movement of the fingers that would result if they were alternated in this situation. Since the first finger to play lands on the next string, it would have to be suddenly lifted back up in order for the second finger to play the next note. Any sudden movement of this kind compromises fluidity of play and adversely affects chops, endurance, tone and relaxed performance.

[NOTE: Alternating fingers tends to be more comfortable than raking in situations involving back-and-forth alternation between adjacent strings (i.e. D A D A D A etc.). It is also preferable to assign the middle finger to the upper string in this situation (see **String Skipping**).]

EXERCISE: *ALTERNATING FINGERS AND RAKING*

For alternating fingers and raking, practice any scales that involve movement from string to string. To begin with, practice a G major scale, ascending and descending, playing the octave note once and alternating between these two fingerings [i= index, m=middle]:

G	A	B	C	D	E	F#	G	F#	E	D	C	B	A	G
i	m	i	m	i	m	i	m	i	m̲	m̲	i	m̲	m̲	i
									RAKE			RAKE		
m	i	m	i	m	i	m	i	i̲	i̲	m	i̲	i̲	m	
									RAKE			RAKE		

Fingers are consistently alternated, except when raking on descending strings (notes E to D and B to A).

STRING SKIPPING

When playing a pattern involving non-adjacent strings (i.e., G and A, or D and E), where possible, assign the index finger to the lower string and the middle finger to the upper string, especially when descending (see exercise below).

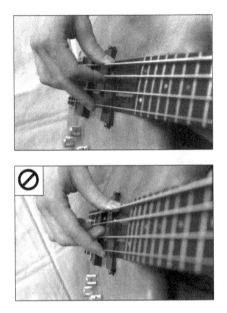

🎵 Since the middle finger is longer, it more naturally extends to the upper string, while the index is naturally positioned above the lower string.

🎵 If the middle finger descends to play the A string after the index has played the G string, it's not at a natural angle to "drag" over the string and must awkwardly descend between the D and A strings to play the string from a lower angle, using more of an inefficient "plucking" motion.

EXERCISE: *STRING SKIPPING*

Here's a string skipping example: version (a) utilizes an awkward fingering, while version (b) is preferable because it assigns the longer (middle) finger to the upper (G) string.

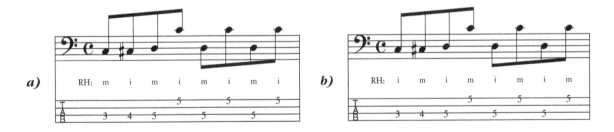

Here's an example of a string skipping lick that involves a possible exception to the alternating fingers rule. In instances such as this, assigning the index to the lower string and the middle to the higher string may be less awkward than alternating fingers.

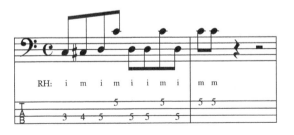

PINKY AND RING FINGERS

a) The pinky and ring fingers move only sympathetically to the index and middle fingers.

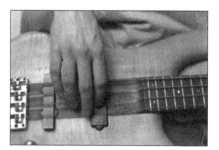

𝄢 Passive, sympathetic movement of fingers requires no energy, whereas holding fingers in a fixed position (either curled under or extended) requires an unnecessary expenditure of energy.

b) The pinky finger rests on the A string when the index and middle fingers play on the G string.

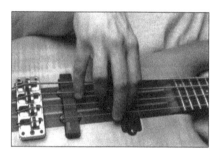

𝄢 Mutes the A string, which is otherwise unprotected from incidental, unwanted ringing or noise during the playing of the G string. Vibration of the A string can result from the slightest touch, especially after the D string is played.

[NOTE: Left-hand fingers may sometimes mute the A string during the playing of the G string, especially in situations involving alternation between the G and A or G and E strings.]

𝄢 The pinky is positioned to rest on the A string without much movement or effort, whereas the ring finger is naturally located over the D string (not the A string) during play on the G string.

EXERCISE: *PINKY MUTING TECHNIQUE*

To practice pinky muting, you need to play things that bring your pinky finger in and out of muting position. Therefore, any patterns involving the G and D strings will do the trick. Here's one to try that you can move up and down the neck. Remember to keep your pinky relaxed while playing on the D string and bring it down lightly to the A string during the playing of the G string.

RIGHT WRIST & FOREARM

a) The wrist and forearm should be relaxed during play.

> **𝄢** Allows energy to be focused on finger movement and contributes to general relaxation. For maximum efficiency, muscle work should be limited to those muscles needed for playing technique (i.e., in your fingers).

b) The forearm should be allowed to rest on the top of the body of the bass.

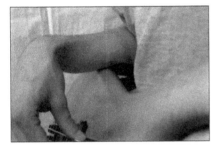

> **𝄢** Relieves the arm from muscle work and allows energy to be focused on finger movements.

> **𝄢** Puts the hand in a natural, relaxed position for playing.
> [NOTE: This may be difficult or awkward with odd-shaped basses such as Flying V's, Explorers and Steinbergers.]

c) The strap should be adjusted so that the bass is in the same position during play whether sitting or standing.

> **𝄢** Allows for consistency of technique between standing and sitting positions.

⇒ If the strap is low, in standing position the forearm cannot rest on the bass and the hand position is affected adversely, with the fingers too parallel to the bass and the thumb forced under the E string (see also *Direction of Finger Movement*, b).

⇒ If the strap is high, a strain is put on the right arm and shoulder which must cramp up in order to position the forearm over the body of the bass. Also, the fingers are put into too much of a "plucking" position (see also *Direction of Finger Movement*, c).

LEFT HAND

THUMB POSITION

a) The thumb provides an anchor for the left hand and should be positioned flat against the back of the neck, opposite to the middle of the hand position.

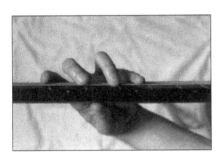

> 𝄢 Once again, using the "opposable thumb" position, the thumb provides a focal point, enabling the fingers to press the strings down against the frets. Without having the thumb in this position, the fingers would be unable to effectively fret notes.

> 𝄢 The thumb anchors the hand, allowing it to be relaxed and increasing control of finger movement.

> 𝄢 The thumb provides a "balance" for all left-hand finger activity when it is centered in the middle of the hand position.

b) Hooking the thumb over the top of the neck should be avoided, except in conjunction with bending, vibrato and sliding techniques.

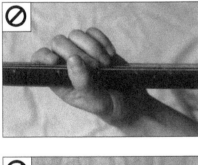

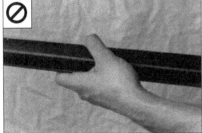

> 𝄢 The thumb is not required for the muting of the E string (see Right Hand *Thumb Position*).

> 𝄢 In this position, the thumb does not support the fretting action of the fingers.

> 𝄢 Hooking the thumb over the top of the neck relieves the wrist from tendon strain, but is not practical in most playing situations because it compromises the flexibility of left-hand fingering.

> 𝄢 Exceptions to this include bending and vibrato, in which case the string is being pushed "upwards" towards the E string, so the thumb is required to be positioned relative to that axis (see *String-bending and Vibrato*).

SPACING OF FINGERS

a) In most music, especially music based on diatonic scales, modes, triads and arpeggios, the left-hand fingers fit most efficiently into four-fret positions, where one finger is assigned to each fret in that position and plays every note that comes up on that fret, no matter what string.

- Using all left-hand fingers spreads out the work, economizes motion and allows for greater speed, endurance and flexibility.

- Once strength is built up in the naturally weaker fingers (especially the pinky) through practice and experience, they are able to become equal partners in left-hand fingering.

b) Up at the top of the neck, especially past the 16th fret, it may sometimes be preferable to shift to a slightly angled position, omitting use of the pinky.

- At the top of the neck, the frets are much closer to each other, making it harder to fit into "one finger per fret" positions.

- When the left arm is angled across the front of the body (as it is when the left hand is at the top of the neck), the hand is more relaxed with the knuckles angled towards the headstock. This removes the pinky from playing position.

c) For simple bass parts involving few notes, the hand position can be relaxed slightly, especially lower on the neck.

- Relaxing the hand position when playing simple patterns, box shapes (e.g. ▦) and single note pedals puts less strain on the left hand.

- In these situations, not all of the fingers need to be in "ready position" if you know only one or two will be needed.

d) Bending, vibrato, sliding, double–stopping and chording techniques involve less spread-out left-hand positions.

- Some techniques require the fretting finger to be supported by the other fingers in a more bunched-up position.

FINGER/STRING CONTACT

a) Strings are fretted using the "flat" area at the ends of the fingers. Though the middle and ring fingers use more of the "tip" since they are longer fingers, an arched hand position should be avoided.

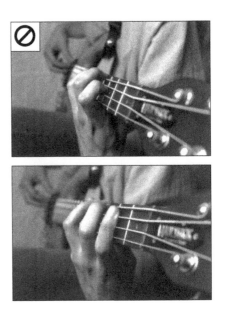

🎵 Using the finger tips is less accurate, since less surface area of the finger is being used and the finger tips can fit between the strings and risk missing contact altogether. Using the finger "flats" allows for more variance in the contact location.

🎵 Using the finger tips is less comfortable and creates an extreme flexion of the wrist. This puts an unnecessary strain on the tendon which over time can lead to tendinitis (tendinitis is an inflammation of the tendon sheath and often also of the enclosed tendon, characterized by localized tenderness, pain on movement and some weakness).

For greatest finger strength, keep the wrist flat or slightly flexed. Excessive flexion or extension limits finger motion by stretching the tendons of the long extensor and flexor muscles respectively. Abduction of the wrist also weakens the finger muscles.

Dorothy Bishop, **The Musician as Athlete**

ᴥ Using the very tips of the fingers restricts the span of reach of the left hand. The fingers can stretch wider in a "flat" position.

ᴥ Using the finger flats puts the fingers in a ready position for barring (see *Barring*).

ᴥ When the fretting finger is arched it must collapse in order to execute barring technique.

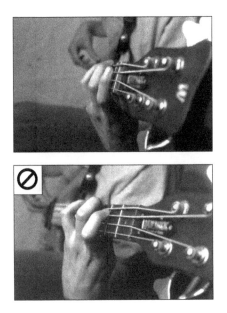

🎵 Using the finger flats allows the fingers to remain close to the strings and to participate in the muting process (see *Left-Hand Muting*).

🎵 Using the finger tips leaves the upper strings unprotected from unwanted noise and open-string ringing.

[NOTE: Playing in an arched position is stronger if the wrist is straight and unflexed; for example, when the thumb is curled over the top of the neck for bending or vibrato. However, when the hand is in regular playing position with the thumb flat behind the neck and the wrist flexed, arching the fingers loses its advantage of strength because it causes such an increase of strain on the tendon.]

b) When using vibrato, bending, pull-off or polyphonic techniques, more of the finger tips should be used to contact the strings.

🎵 Techniques such as bending and vibrato require extra strength, which is provided by using the tips. [NOTE: This extra strength and control is achieved only when the thumb is positioned over the neck, causing the wrist to be unflexed.]

🎵 Using the finger tips avoids contact and friction between the finger and the fretboard, facilitating the moving of the string up and down parallel to the frets (see *String-bending and Vibrato*).

🎵 When playing pull-offs, the fretting finger of the first note needs to be arched in order to "play" the second note by pulling down on the string on an axis parallel to the frets (see *Hammer-Ons and Pull-Offs*).

🎵 Polyphonic techniques require many muting functions to be suspended, since more than one string is required to vibrate at the same time. Arching the fingers in these situations ensures that strings will not be muted by the left-hand index finger.

LEFT-HAND MUTING

a) The index finger rests over the top of the strings above (higher in pitch than) the one being played, muting them. Only contact is required; the index should not press the string down to the frets unless it is playing a note.

𝄢 The strings above (higher in pitch than) the one being played cannot be muted by the right hand and the muting process must be thorough in order to prevent unwanted ringing and string noise.

𝄢 The index is comfortably positioned over the strings and requires very little energy to make contact.

𝄢 Since the index finger is located at the headstock extremity of the hand position, it can never interfere with the free vibration of notes fretted by the other fingers.

𝄢 In cases where the index is the fretting finger, it can still mute the strings above the one being fretted.

b) In some situations, other left-hand fingers may become involved in muting just from being positioned close above the strings. For example, when playing a C major arpeggio (C,E,G,C) starting on the 3rd fret of the A string, the pinky mutes the G string as it frets the perfect 5th on the D string.

𝄢 There are often situations where strings are being muted by more than one finger. Generally, the more muting that can be done without compromising playing technique, the better protected you are from unwanted open string ringing and fret noise.

FINGER POSITION

a) Fingers should remain within approximately ½ cm or ¼ in. above the string.

🎵 Removing any fingers from their playing position involves unnecessary movement and detracts from the efficiency of play in the left hand. The closer the fingers are to where they have played and will play, the less movement is required. This saves energy and contributes to speed and endurance.

b) Fingers should remain parallel to the frets and in position as much as possible.

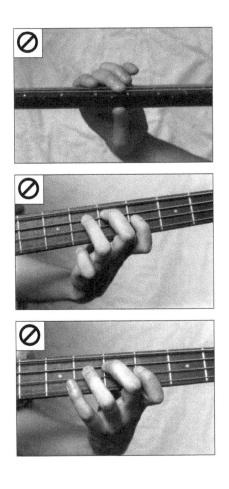

🎵 Taking fingers out of position, especially pulling the pinky down and towards the headstock, slows down left-hand fingering technique and tires the hand.

🎵 However, some techniques such as bending, vibrato, sliding, double-stops, harmonics and chording may necessitate a more "removed" pinky position (see *Spacing of Fingers*, d).

FRETTING POSITION

Fingers should depress the string just to the left (headstock side) of the fret to be played.

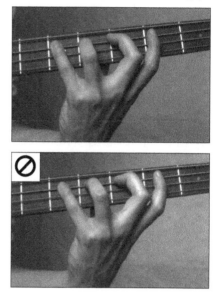

⨠ Playing close to the fret results in better intonation and less fret noise.

⨠ Less energy is required to hold down the string.

FINGER PRESSURE

The fingers of the left hand apply sufficient pressure against the fingerboard to make solid contact with the frets, but no more than necessary.

⨠ Applying insufficient pressure with the left-hand fingers will result in excessive fret noise and poor tone quality.

⨠ Applying more pressure than is necessary to close the note is a waste of energy and will adversely affect dexterity, speed and endurance.

ASCENDING ON ONE STRING

In ascending patterns on one string, fingers should remain in contact with the string after fretting notes. Fingers "behind" the fretting finger need only touch the string, applying very little pressure.

[e.g. For playing a G, A, B♭ sequence on the E string starting with the index finger at the third fret: keep the index in contact with the string while fretting the A with the ring finger, and keep the index and ring fingers in contact with the string while fretting the B♭ with the pinky finger.]

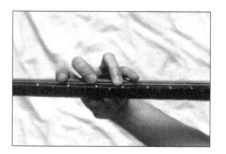

⨠ Keeping more than one finger in contact with the string prevents accidental harmonics (see *Playing Harmonics*). It also reduces fret noise and ensures that the open string won't sound between the playing of fretted notes.

[e.g. Play a C at the 5th fret of the G string, then lift your fretting finger, leaving no fingers in contact with the string. You'll hear a harmonic (G) as the finger leaves the fretboard, followed by the open string G once the finger has left the string.]

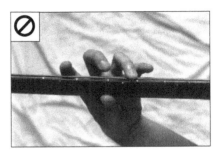

♪ Lifting fingers off the string after fretting notes requires more energy than leaving them down.

TRANSITIONS BETWEEN HAND POSITIONS

a) As much as possible, the fingers of the left hand should "anticipate" moves and shifts of position.

♪ Minimizing sudden movements by spreading out movement over time is more energy-efficient and results in greater flexibility, speed and endurance. It also helps prevent fast or complex licks from sounding sloppy.

b) **INCHWORMING**
One of the most efficient ways of changing positions in the left hand can be referred to as "inchworming." It involves expanding and contracting the hand position in a way that gradually propels the hand up or down the neck (see exercise on p. 40). Inchworming can be done during play on any string or any combination of strings.

♪ Inchworming allows the hand to be in gradual, continual motion instead of suddenly moving the whole position.

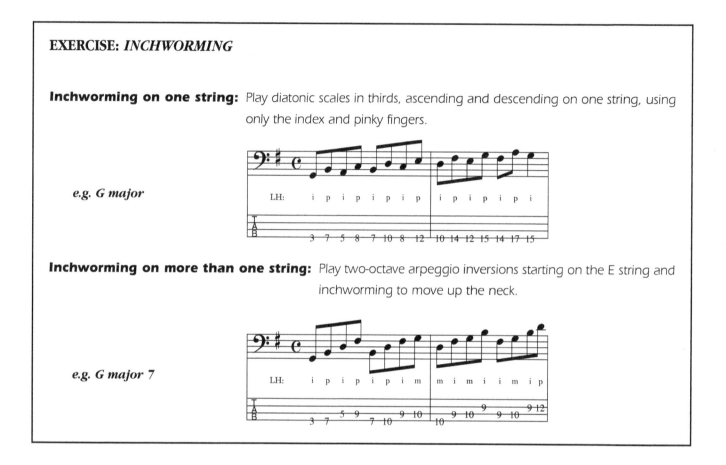

EXERCISE: *INCHWORMING*

Inchworming on one string: Play diatonic scales in thirds, ascending and descending on one string, using only the index and pinky fingers.

e.g. G major

Inchworming on more than one string: Play two-octave arpeggio inversions starting on the E string and inchworming to move up the neck.

e.g. G major 7

c) In some cases, moving the whole hand is necessary, though it should be avoided where possible.

> **𝄢** Some wide interval jumps simply require the whole hand to make a sudden movement (especially intervals larger than an octave and a half; for example, from the G at the 3rd fret on the E string to the G at the 12th fret on the G string).

> **𝄢** Especially when improvising, musical ideas tend to jump ahead of technical foresight; sudden decisions require sudden movement.

d) Positions can be changed with a very legato effect by sliding the fretting finger from one fret to another. Any finger can be used to slide up or down the neck.

> **𝄢** For long slides and slides followed by bending or vibrato, using the ring finger in a "bunched-up" hand position with the thumb over the neck results in the greatest strength and control (see *String Bending and Vibrato*).

BARRING

a) When ascending strings on one fret, for example, from the 5th fret on the D string to the 5th fret on the G string, the fretting finger should not be lifted between notes. The end part of the finger flat should fret the first note (G), and the pressure point should shift to further down the finger for the fretting of the second, higher note (C). The fretting finger always mutes the top string while playing the bottom string and vice versa. Barring can be executed by any finger on any two adjacent strings.

🎵 Lifting the finger from string to string requires an unnecessary expenditure of energy and is very slow.

🎵 Barring keeps the transition between strings clean and quiet by incorporating a muting function.

b) To play a perfect fourth as a double stop (harmonically), the finger is depressed on both strings at the same time and the fingers of the right hand play both notes simultaneously.

🎵 Both strings must be fretted at once in order to ring simultaneously.

🎵 Fretting both strings with one finger keeps the hand in position and requires less movement.

EXERCISE: *BARRING*

In four-finger patterns: Start with the G and D strings for this exercise and move the pattern up and down the neck. When it gets easy, move it to the D and A strings and finally, to the A and E strings. Make sure that you don't let any of the notes overlap.

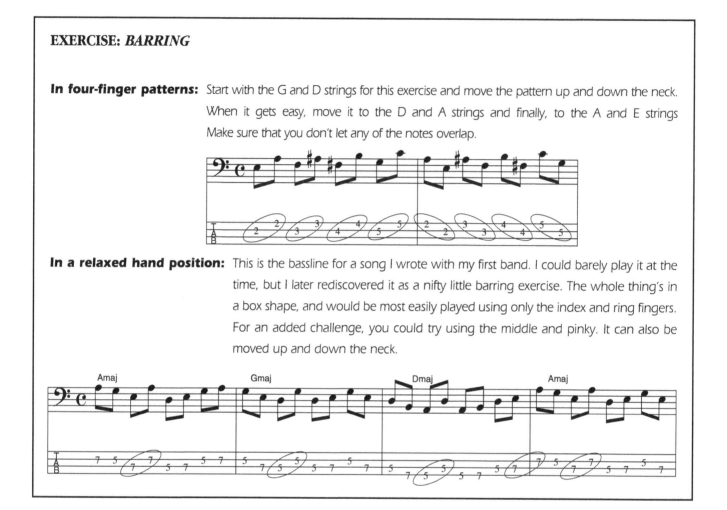

In a relaxed hand position: This is the bassline for a song I wrote with my first band. I could barely play it at the time, but I later rediscovered it as a nifty little barring exercise. The whole thing's in a box shape, and would be most easily played using only the index and ring fingers. For an added challenge, you could try using the middle and pinky. It can also be moved up and down the neck.

HAMMER-ONS AND PULL-OFFS

HAMMER-ONS

Ascending by semitone, tone or tone-and-a-half steps* can be achieved without articulating two separate notes with the right hand. One finger frets the first note and then another "hammers on" the second against the fret.

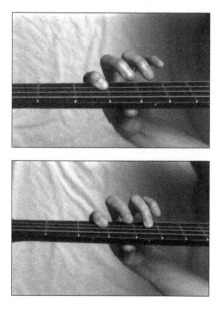

𝄢 Hammer-ons result in greater speed because the right hand has less notes to play. The sound produced is also more legato than can be achieved when each note played is articulated by the right hand.

*[NOTE: Larger intervals can be played using hammer-ons and pull-offs, especially when hammering on from (or pulling off to) an open string.]

PULL-OFFS

Pull-offs are the opposite of hammer-ons, and are achieved by playing the string with the fretting finger of the first note. Instead of lifting up normally, the fretting finger pulls downwards, playing the string. To achieve this, the fretting finger of the first note has to be in an "arched" position (see *Finger/String Contact*, b).

[NOTE: "Ornaments" that can be produced with hammer-ons and pull-offs include trills, acciaccaturas, appoggiaturas and mordents. For full descriptions of these techniques and exercises for practicing them, consult **Slur, Ornament and Reach Development Exercises** by Aaron Shearer.]

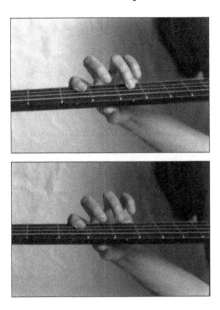

𝄢 Pull-offs result in greater speed because the right hand has less notes to play. The sound produced is also more legato than can be achieved when each note played is articulated by the right hand.

[NOTE: Hammer-ons and pull-offs result in less consistent tone and volume than articulating every note. They should therefore be used only when required for legato effects or speed.]

EXERCISE: *HAMMER-ONS and PULL-OFFS*

A good exercise to practice hammer-ons: Start with semitones, using the index and middle fingers. Hammer-on with the index from open E to F, open A to B♭, open D to E♭, open G to A♭. Then fret A♭ (1st fret G string) with the index and hammer-on to A with the middle finger, E♭ (1st fret D string) to E, B♭ (1st fret A string) to B and F (1st fret E string) to G♭. Move up and down the neck in this pattern.

Repeat the exercise with tones (major seconds) and minor third intervals.

To practice pull-offs, just turn the exercise around (i.e., pull-off F to E, B♭ to A, etc.)

For a bigger challenge, repeat the exercise with the middle and ring fingers, then the ring and pinky fingers.

Trills (rapid alternations of hammer-ons and pull-offs) can also be practiced with this approach.

You can also try "stacking" hammer-ons or pull-offs (i.e. for hammer-ons, hammer E to F to F# , A to A# to B, etc.)

STRING BENDING AND VIBRATO

STRING BENDING

String bending is most efficiently achieved by hooking the thumb over the top of the neck, fretting a note with the tip of a finger (usually the ring or middle) and pushing the string against the fret and up towards the thumb.

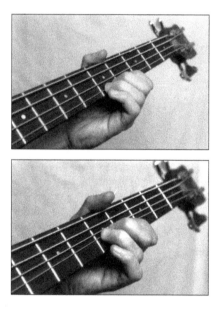

🎵 String bending and vibrato techniques on a fretted instrument require the string to change contact position with the fret in order to effect a change of pitch. To achieve this, the thumb has to oppose the finger "push" by being positioned over the top of the neck.

EXERCISE: *STRING BENDING*

The trickiest thing about string bending is intonation. If you bend a note and you don't bend it to an accurate pitch that works with the music, you'll make some ugly sounds and possibly enemies as well (Remember, guitarists see this as their domain, so if you do it badly, they'll be down your throat in a second).

In order to develop an accurate bending technique, start with semitone and tone bends mid-way up the neck. First, normally play an F at the 10th fret on the G string, followed by a G one tone up. Then, using more of the tip of the ring finger, grouping your fingers together for support and hooking the thumb over the top of the neck, fret the F note and push it up towards the thumb until you attain the pitch of the G note. By alternating between fretting the G and bending up to it, you should be able to train yourself to keep your bending in tune.

Try bending up semitones, bending on other strings and adding vibrato to the end of each bend. For a more advanced exercise, try playing scales up and down one string in 2nds, always bending to the next note (i.e., for C major starting at the 5th fret on the G string: bend C to D, then D to E, E to F, F to G, etc.). Remember, string bending is infinitely easier with light-gauge strings.

VIBRATO

Vibrato is achieved in the same position as string bending, with the fretting finger moving up and down in order to oscillate or "vibrate" the pitch. Vibrato can be slow or fast, wide or narrow, depending on the desired effect.

Bending and vibrato require more strength than normal fretting technique. The ring finger tends to work best for vibrato because it can be supported by the middle and index fingers, which are not in a position to interfere with the free vibration of the string. Also the left-hand thumb should be hooked over the top of the neck (see *String Bending*, p. 44).

PLAYING HARMONICS

To play a harmonic, a finger of the left hand touches the string above a fret and the right hand plays the string normally. Contact must be made at only one place on the string by one finger in order for a harmonic to sound. The clearest harmonics are located at the 4th, 5th, 7th and 12th frets, but there are many more all over the neck.

[NOTE: For details on the science of sound and playing harmonics, check out **Bass Harmonics**, by Dean Peer]

EXERCISE: *HARMONICS*

If you've never played harmonics before, the best way to start is by learning how to **tune** using harmonics. Touch the G string at the 7th fret (with any finger) without pressing it down and play the string normally with the right hand. You should hear a harmonic. Next, arch the left-hand fingers and, without muting the G string, play the 5th fret harmonic on the D string. The two harmonics should be at the same pitch. If you hear rhythmic "beats" or pulses, you're not in tune. In order to tune the D string to the G string, turn the tuning peg for the D string until the beats slow down and the two strings ring in unison. If the beats are speeding up, you're turning in the wrong direction. Repeat the process for the other strings (7th fret D string and 5th fret A string, then 7th fret A string and 5th fret E string).

LEFT ARM POSITION

The left arm should simply hang relaxed, with the elbow loose and separated from the side of the body.

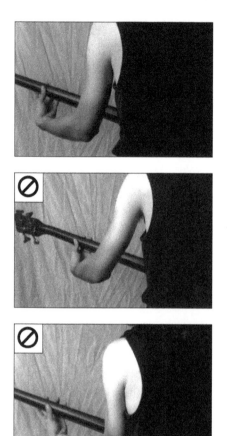

𝄢 Straining the left arm in any way detracts from the strength and coordination of left-hand movements and is a waste of energy.

𝄢 Digging the left elbow into the side of the ribs is a waste of energy and leads to strained and rigid hand movements.

THE QUASI-CHROMATIC **EXERCISE**

This is a good set of all-purpose exercises, especially useful for the left hand. It's called "quasi-chromatic" because of its similarity to the chromatic scale.

The quasi-chromatic exercise is versatile because it's a relatively simple pattern that uses all the fingers equally, includes all aspects of basic technique and involves all strings and the whole fretboard. When practicing it, try moving up and down the neck as far as possible in both directions.

When practicing this exercise, consider the following:

- **Spacing of Fingers** (are you assigning a finger to each fret?)
- **Finger/String Contact** (are you using the finger flats and keeping the wrist relaxed?)
- **Left-hand Muting** (are you muting the strings above the one being played, using the index?)
- **Ascending on One String** (are you keeping the fingers down after fretting notes?)
- **Finger Distance from Strings/Hand Position** (are you keeping your hand perpendicular to the neck and are your fingers in position and always ready to play?)
- **Fretting Position** (are you depressing the strings just to the left of the frets?)
- **Finger Pressure** (are you applying enough pressure to get clean tone, but not wasting energy?)

For further technical challenge and some weird melodies, try substituting the "1234" pattern notated above with any of these permutations:

1234	2134	3124	4123
1243	2143	3142	4132
1324	2314	3214	4213
1342	2341	3241	4231
1423	2413	3412	4312
1432	2431	3421	4321

For all of the above aspects of technique, practicing diatonic scales is also useful; but remember that when focusing on specific aspects of technique, it's preferable to stick to simple patterns and scales that you know well, and that won't distract you too much from the task at hand. If you always have to be consciously thinking about what note comes next, you won't have enough attention available for technique.

MUTING **SUMMARY**

Generally, the left hand is responsible for muting the strings above (higher in pitch than) the one being played; and the right hand is responsible for muting the strings below (lower in pitch than) the one being played.

When playing on the G string

The index and middle fingers of the right hand mute the D string with every note played, the right-hand pinky mutes the A string and the right-hand thumb mutes the E string. In some situations, left-hand fingers may mute the A string during play on the G string.

When playing on the D string

The left-hand index finger mutes the G string, the index and middle fingers of the right hand mute the A string with every note played and the right-hand thumb mutes the E string.

When playing on the A string

The left hand index finger mutes the G and D strings, the index and middle fingers of the right hand mute the E string with every note played and the E string may also be muted by the right-hand thumb.

When playing on the E string

The left hand index finger mutes the G, D and A strings.

Muting Summary for 5-String Bass

The technique summarized above applies for the bottom four strings (D, A, E, B) of the 5-string bass; i.e., G = D, D = A, A = E, E = B. When playing on the G string, the index and middle fingers of the right hand mute the D string with every note played, the right-hand ring finger mutes the A string, the right-hand pinky mutes the E string and the right-hand thumb mutes the B string. In some situations, left-hand fingers may mute the A and E strings during play on the G string.

Muting Summary for 6-String Bass

Muting technique for 5-string applies for the bottom five strings of the 6-string bass. When playing on the C string, the index and middle fingers of the right hand mute the G string with every note played, the right-hand ring finger mutes the D string, the right-hand pinky mutes the A string and the right-hand thumb moves to rest on the E string, muting the E string and the B string at the same time. In some situations, left-hand fingers may mute the D, A and E strings during play on the C string.

I wish you good luck in developing solid, efficient technique. If you ingrain good habits,

technique will become your servant, not your master. Happy practicing!